Bible reflect

for older people

BRF
Ministries

 Ministries

15 The Chambers, Vineyard,
Abingdon OX14 3FE
+44 (0)1865 319700 | brf.org.uk

Bible Reading Fellowship is a charity (233280)
and company limited by guarantee (301324),
registered in England and Wales

ISBN 978 1 80039 254 0

Acknowledgements
Scripture quotations marked with the following abbreviations are taken from the version shown. NRSV: The New Revised Standard Version Updated Edition. Copyright © 2021 National Council of Churches of Christ in the United States of America. Used by permission. All rights reserved worldwide. NIV: The Holy Bible, New International Version, Anglicised edition, copyright © 1979, 1984, 2011 by Biblica. Used by permission of Hodder & Stoughton Publishers, a Hachette UK company. All rights reserved. 'NIV' is a registered trademark of Biblica. UK trademark number 1448790. NEB: The New English Bible, copyright © Cambridge University Press and Oxford University Press 1961, 1970. All rights reserved. NLT: The Holy Bible, New Living Translation, copyright © 1996, 2004, 2007, 2013. Used by permission of Tyndale House Publishers, Inc., Carol Stream, Illinois 60188. All rights reserved. TLB: The Living Bible copyright © 1971 by Tyndale House Foundation. Used by permission of Tyndale House Publishers Inc., Carol Stream, Illinois 60188. All rights reserved.

Every effort has been made to trace and contact copyright owners for material used in this resource. We apologize for any inadvertent omissions or errors, and would ask those concerned to contact us so that full acknowledgement can be made in the future.

A catalogue record for this book is available from the British Library

Printed and bound in the UK by Zenith Media NP4 0DQ

Contents

About the writers

Lynn Goslin was born in Edinburgh and brought up in the Scottish Episcopal Church. She acquired a degree in linguistics and English language before training as a speech and language therapist. Her first marriage took her, as a vicar's wife, to the diocese of Yukon in Canada for a few years and then to parishes in Norfolk and Yorkshire. She's a home group leader and ardent bell ringer at her church in North Yorkshire.

Roger Combes has served in a variety of parishes in London, Cambridge and Hastings. Before retiring he was archdeacon of Horsham. He and his wife, Christine, now live in Crawley, near Gatwick airport. They have two daughters and a small, energetic grandson.

Clare O'Driscoll worked in Bible translation administration for 13 years before leaving for a more freelance life. Since then, she has been giving Spanish and French tuition and writing occasional articles for Christian publications. She is also part of the team of volunteer editors at *Magnet* magazine. She loves the sea and is currently working on a writing project about beach cafés. Clare lives in West Sussex with her family.

Emlyn Williams worked for Scripture Union for many years, in various places and roles, particularly relating to schools. He is a writer of many individual and group Bible materials. Following three years working with an Anglican church in Southampton, he retired and now lives in Norfolk, where he continues to write.

From the Editor

Welcome

Walking near my home one day, a tiny hazelnut bounced off my head and into the tangle of brambles at the side of the track. So small and new, the nut was bone white, with a spikey green ruff. Rolling it on my palm, I thought of Chicken Licken, who was convinced the sky was falling in when an acorn landed on her head. She rushed around, spreading panic about an imagined catastrophe, like so many lurid social media campaigns today. It did not end well.

Many of the reflections in this issue are, by contrast, about good endings: about how keeping faith in the face of real problems and catastrophes, large and small, can make us in some way deeper, stronger, more peaceful.

One of the most enduring encouragements to faith and trust in God comes to us from the 14th-century mystic, Mother Julian of Norwich. In her *Revelations of Divine Love*, she recalled contemplating 'a little thing the size of a hazel nut' in the palm of her hand. She wrote:

'I looked at it with my mind's eye and I thought, "What can this be?" And the answer came, "It is all that is made." I marvelled that it could last, for I thought it might have crumbled to nothing, it was so small. And the answer came into my mind, "It lasts and ever shall because God loves it."'

Go well

Using these reflections

Perhaps you have always had a special time each day for reading the Bible and praying. But now, as you grow older, you are finding it more difficult to keep to a regular pattern or find it harder to concentrate. Or, maybe you've never done this before. Whatever your situation, these Bible reflections aim to help you take a few moments to read God's Word and pray whenever you have time or feel that would be helpful.

When to read them

You might use these Bible reflections in the morning or last thing at night, but they work at any time of day. There are 40 reflections here, grouped around four themes, by four different writers. Each one includes some verses from the Bible, a reflection to help you in your own thinking about God, and a prayer suggestion. The reflections aren't dated, so it doesn't matter if you don't want to read every day. The Bible verses are printed, but you might prefer to follow them in your own Bible.

How to read them

- **Take time** to quieten yourself, becoming aware of God's presence, asking him to speak to you through the Bible and the reflection.

- **Read** the Bible verses and the reflection:
  - What do you especially like or find helpful in these verses?
  - What might God be saying to you through this reading?
  - Is there something to pray about or thank God for?

- **Pray.** Each reflection includes a prayer suggestion. You might like to pray for yourself or take the opportunity to think about and pray for others.

Conversations with Jesus

Lynn Goslin

In my previous work as a speech and language therapist, I spent hours listening to, transcribing and dissecting conversations between people. The skills of listening, turn-taking, relevance, grammar and speech never cease to amaze me, and it is no wonder that, for many people, communication is difficult or unsuccessful.

In this series I have 'listened to' conversations between Jesus and individuals where both sides' contributions have been 'transcribed' by the gospel writers. What surprised me is not so much Jesus' graciousness and sensitivity, his quickness of perception and his understanding of the human situation, but rather the way in which he draws out from the other person their deepest and truest selves, accepts them as they are and leads them on to think differently.

We too have our own conversations with this same Jesus: sometimes they seem one-sided, fraught with difficulty in expressing our complex needs and feelings. These gospel conversations assure us that Jesus seeks us out as individuals and meets us where we are and as we are.

If possible, take time to read the entire conversation for each reflection, given next to the Bible reference.

John 4:17–18 (NRSV, abridged)
Full conversation: John 4:5–30

Getting to the truth

**The woman answered him, 'I have no husband.' Jesus said to her...
'What you have said is true!'**

It was a family joke that my father, left on a seat while we went shopping, would invariably be chatting with a total stranger on our return.

Jesus starts this conversation with the unnamed woman at the well by simply requesting a drink; what follows is a full-blown debate about honesty before God. The woman does everything to deflect attempts to delve into the truth of her life; she brings out all the divisive stereotypes – Jew versus Samaritan, male versus female, differing religious history and practices. But at each deflection Jesus presses her to face and acknowledge her truth.

Finally, a direct challenge from Jesus results in her first honest response, 'I have no husband', which Jesus acknowledges as true. Again she resorts to distraction – worship here, or in Jerusalem? – but Jesus returns the focus to her relationship with God who is to be worshipped in spirit and, tellingly, in truth. Her eventual honesty is rewarded by Jesus' own honesty: for the first time he openly admits his Messianic role: 'I am he'.

As our conversations with Jesus deepen, we find ourselves confronting uncomfortable truths. Only then do we understand, not only that he knows everything that we have ever done, but that he does not turn away.

■ **PRAYER**

Lord, help me to face my uncomfortable truths and know your loving acceptance. Amen

Luke 19:4–5 (NRSV, abridged)
Full conversation: Luke 19:1–10

Trying to see

[Zacchaeus] ran ahead… to see him, because he was going to pass that way… [Jesus] looked up and said to him, 'Zacchaeus, hurry and come down, for I must stay at your house today.'

At a recent pop concert my daughter was thrilled to be picked out of the 21,000-strong crowd and shown on the on-stage screen, chatting with the star herself. 'She loved my bright pink top, Mum!'

Imagine Zacchaeus, caught up in the crowd's excitement but unable to see, climbing up a tree (probably uncomfortably) to then be noticed and addressed by the 'star' out of all the people amassed there. For Zacchaeus, right time, right place.

It wasn't totally by luck, however; he had worked at this: 'he was trying to see who Jesus was' and he followed the lead of his restless heart, working out Jesus' probable route and overcoming the problem of seeing over the crowd. He placed himself at the scene, and Jesus responded with the challenge 'I must stay at your house' – not a fleeting encounter but one that will change Zacchaeus' life. He in turn rises to the challenge and finds that, while he thought he was searching for Jesus, Jesus was searching for him: 'The Son of Man came to seek out and to save the lost.'

Sometimes, when we feel lost, all we need to do is sit – physically, mentally, emotionally and sometimes uncomfortably – in the place where we are most likely to be met by the one who seeks us.

■ **PRAYER**
Lord, stay at my house today. Amen

Luke 10:40–42 (NRSV, abridged)
Full conversation: Luke 10:38–42

Choosing the better part

'My sister has left me to do all the work…' But the Lord answered her, 'Martha, Martha, you are worried and distracted by many things, but few things are needed – indeed only one. Mary has chosen the better part, which will not be taken away from her.'

A friend and I often discuss this encounter between Jesus and the sisters, Martha and Mary. As extroverts, we feel aggrieved that Mary is commended over Martha for choosing 'the better part'. Doesn't Jesus want someone to make dinner?

The answer lies perhaps in the word 'distracted': Martha is the welcomer and preparer of home and food, and these are entirely excellent activities. Following Brother Lawrence, they are vehicles for practising the presence of God and exercising love in everyday life. It's just that 'doing' can become a life habit that crowds out or distracts us from 'being'. If we are constantly planning the next event, filling our time with activity, we can become distracted from simply being in the presence of God and hearing the 'still small voice', as Brother Lawrence termed it.

James 1:22 urges us to be 'doers of the word and not merely hearers'. We must first place ourselves at the feet of Jesus to be 'hearers', giving time and silent attention, listening to God's promptings, reflecting, absorbing his presence. From that place can we then do.

In my experience, doing this is infinitely more challenging than many of the items on my daily to-do list.

■ **PRAYER**

Lord, turn me from being distracted to being with you, then let me do your work. Amen

John 20:16 (NRSV)
Full conversation: John 20:11–18

Called by name

Jesus said to her, 'Mary!' She turned and said to him in Hebrew, 'Rabbouni!' (which means Teacher).

Recognising faces is not my strong point. I have waved cheerfully at complete strangers believing I know them and then failed to spot a friend passing in the street.

In this case, Mary enters this conversation with a preconception: she knows that Jesus is dead. Her upset and indignation at the apparent removal of his precious body colours her meeting with this man in the garden. His question, 'Whom are you looking for?', reveals in her answer that she is looking for the wrong thing: 'Tell me where you have laid him.'

But Jesus' unadorned use of her name, a symbol of being known and, in this case, loved, brings instant recognition, and turns Mary round and allows her to look at the right thing. In 'Rabbouni!' (the intensive form of 'Teacher') we hear all the wonder, joy and relief that come from seeing the worst disaster in the world resolved and made right.

That moment will stay in her memory, but she is not to cling to it because there is work to be done. However, that simple 'Mary' will resonate in her heart forever.

■ PRAYER

Lord, you call me to turn and look at you. Help me to recognise you and carry that wonder with me in the world. Amen

Luke 24:17 (NRSV)
Full conversation: Luke 24:13–35

Accompanied on the journey

[Jesus] said to them, 'What are you discussing with each other while you walk along?' They stood still, looking sad.

Many people, me included, find that a good walk can help to sort out thoughts and feelings: with body movement and distracting surroundings, busy thoughts come into alignment, problems are put into perspective and sometimes resolved.

Not so for the two people on the Emmaus Road. They find themselves churning over the sad events of the crucifixion and the puzzling experience of the empty tomb. Into their confusion and sadness steps the 'stranger' whose question opens up the flood of hurt and sorrow that blinds them to seeing the truth before them. Jesus' response is a challenge – 'how slow of heart to believe' – but by the time he has 'interpreted to them the things about himself' their hearts are 'burning within them'. Jesus satisfies their intellectual need to understand, their hearts are able to respond and the conversation turns them round metaphorically and literally: they make the seven-mile hike back to Jerusalem to share their revelation.

On our life's walk, Jesus challenges us to open our hearts to him, acknowledging what blinds us. Only then can he restore us so that our hearts 'burn within us' with renewed belief and purpose.

■ PRAYER
Lord, help me to open my heart to you entirely and renew my belief.
Amen

John 21:21–22 (NRSV, abridged)
Full conversation: John 21:15–22

Follow me

[Peter] said to Jesus, 'Lord, what about him?' Jesus said... 'What is that to you? Follow me!'

The way of the world is often to encourage comparison with others, seeking to match or outdo them in exams, success, wealth or importance. Envy, self-doubt, feelings of grievance or failure are often the result.

When Jesus calls Peter to a private conversation on the lakeshore, Peter's three declarations of love are traditionally interpreted as counterbalancing his three-times denial. This prepares the forgiven Peter for his task of feeding Jesus' sheep. Jesus outlines the martyrdom to come and calls him to the simply phrased but so difficult task: 'Follow me.'

Throughout, Peter typically makes his responses with genuine feeling and perhaps some exasperation: he does love Jesus, he will feed his sheep. He is turned to Jesus, ready to follow. But then he looks away from Jesus and sees 'the disciple whom Jesus loved.'* Perhaps still a little ruffled from Jesus' insistent questions and the description of his fate, he feels a rush of what? – curiosity? envy? pique? Jesus will not answer the question; as C.S. Lewis says through the mouth of Aslan the lion, 'I am telling you your story, not [theirs]. No one is told any story but their own.'** Peter's work is to follow and to complete his story.

■ PRAYER

Lord, hold my gaze so that, in steadfastly looking at you, my story goes hand in hand with your will. Amen

* Traditionally believed to be John the apostle and evangelist
** C.S. Lewis, *The Horse and His Boy* (Puffin, 1965)

John 1:47b–48a (NRSV)
Full conversation: John 1:43–51

Come and see

[Jesus said of Nathanael] 'Here is truly an Israelite in whom there is no deceit!' Nathanael asked him, 'Where did you get to know me?'

'Och, you'll not like Glasgow!' said an elderly lady at my Edinburgh church as I explained about my impending move. This proved, of course, to be wrong, as so many of our stereotypes tend to be, and Glasgow continues to be one of my all-time favourite cities.

Nathanael's unhelpful reference to town rivalries is challenged by Philip's simple but effective, 'Come and see.' Philip has quickly grasped something in his own encounter with Jesus and wants his friend to share in this.

Jesus' greeting startles Nathanael out of his preconceptions: this unknown preacher declares him to be a man 'in whom there is no deceit' and alludes to what was probably a private time of prayer and meditation in the shade of the fig tree. Nathanael finds himself known in a way that utterly convinces him that he has found the long-awaited Son of God.

This entire conversation happened only because of Philip's witness, sharing his own experience of Jesus and urging Nathanael to see for himself. Nathanael journeys from disbelief to certainty of belief as he finds himself uniquely known by this man from Nazareth.

■ PRAYER

Lord, help me to share my story simply and clearly so that others may come and see you. Amen

John 5:6b (NRSV)
Full conversation: John 5:2–14

The challenge to change

[Jesus] said to him, 'Do you want to be made well?'

'How many churchwardens does it take to change a lightbulb?' runs the old joke. The answer, in an outraged tone, is 'CHANGE??!!' Apologies to churchwardens, because the desire to keep things as they are is known to us all; change challenges our comfortable habits and introduces uncertainty.

Jesus knew this as he considered the man by Beth-zatha pool. 'Do you want to be made well?' as a conversation starter cuts to the heart of the matter: the unnamed man might be used to this life. Change would demand a return to society, making a living, forging relationships, finding new purpose.

The man's answer is clear: he does want change but cannot engineer it himself – 'I have no one.' Again Jesus is direct: circumventing the easy solution – the miraculous pool – He demands faith and action: 'Stand up.' After 38 years this man finds that his will to change, accompanied by Jesus' power, results in a totally new life, albeit with its own challenges, including, in this case, the outraged religious leaders.

Jesus knows our deep-seated desire to be 'well' and loves us for it. All it takes is our will to respond, to stand up and to walk with him.

■ PRAYER

Lord, I am fearful of change and challenge. Help me to stand up and look at you. Amen

Matthew 15:28b (NRSV)
Full conversation: Matthew 15:21–28

Being yourself

Then Jesus answered her, 'Woman, great is your faith! Let it be done for you as you wish.'

Sassy, unfazed, determined, resilient: all words which my daughters would approve of to describe a woman of our time.

Perhaps not so much approved of in first-century Tyre and Sidon, where this shouting Canaanite woman so riles Jesus' disciples that they beg him to send her away. Unlike the Samaritan woman at the well, this woman knows exactly what she is looking for; she has a beloved child who is seriously ill and needs healing.

She enters the scene shouting, gaining attention where a quieter approach might have failed. Jesus does not answer immediately: this sudden encounter with a Gentile challenges the range of his ministry and his eventual answer expresses his dilemma.

Once heard, the woman moves closer, kneels and starts a one-to-one conversation where all that she is cannot be ignored. She couches her need in the simple 'Lord, help me', the cry of all humanity. Unfazed by the reference to 'dogs', she has the wit and presence of mind to turn Jesus' remark back at him; you can almost hear his gasp of sheer delight, not only at her faith, but at the sheer chutzpah of the woman – what the Scottish minister and theologian William Barclay describes as her 'gallant and audacious love'.*

■ PRAYER

Lord, thank you for your delight in us as we are. Amen

* William Barclay, *The Gospel of Mark* Vol. 2 (Saint Andrew Press, 2009)

Luke 7:47a (NRSV)
Full conversation: Luke 7:36–50

Witnessing to God's generosity

'Therefore, I tell you, her many sins have been forgiven; hence she has shown great love.'

In considering these conversations with Jesus, I have been struck by the way an encounter with Jesus reaches right to the heart of things, brushing away our attempted deflections and defences and making us face the truth about ourselves, however well we have hidden it from ourselves and others.

The woman in this conversation is a silent participant but her actions speak louder than words. After the facing of unpalatable truths and subsequent forgiveness comes loving resolution and a revolution, a turning around, a giving away of once-precious things: Zacchaeus gives half of his wealth away, the Samaritan woman bears witness to her neighbours, Mary runs from the garden to tell the disciples the good news, the Emmaus friends walk seven miles back to Jerusalem to witness to the resurrection and Peter gives himself to a martyr's death after faithfully feeding the 'sheep'. All impulsive, generous, overspilling from the hearts that have found living water and cannot help but share it.

■ PRAYER

Father God, grant us such an encounter with our risen Lord that we cannot help but become generous and inspired witnesses, telling our story as a testimony to your generosity and love. Amen

Have faith in God

Roger Combes

Our town centre has had a bit of a facelift. The main square has been repaved, and child-friendly fountains have been installed. The town hall has been demolished and a new glass one has appeared. The gardens now sport a new bandstand and a brightly coloured playground. Even the station has had an upgrade.

From time to time, Christians can feel in need of a bit of a 'faith-lift'. Faith does need to be renewed. Constantly. It's what we see through-out the Bible. There are many fine stories of the faith of God's people, trusting the Lord who called them and saved them. But their faith is rarely consistent. It seems to wax and wane. In the New Testament, disciples are sometimes full of faith, sometimes 'lukewarm'.

Faith is a major theme in the Bible. 'Trust in the Lord with all your heart', says Proverbs 3:5 (NRSV). Jude 20 speaks of building 'yourselves up on your most holy faith' (NRSV). Jesus advised his disciples to 'have faith in God' (Mark 11:22, NRSV). In these reflections we shall look at some references to faith in the Bible, hoping they may give a bit of a lift and renewal to our faith.

Luke 1:37–38a (NRSV)

Mary's faith

[The angel said,] 'For nothing will be impossible with God.' Then Mary said, 'Here I am, the servant of the Lord; let it be with me according to your word.'

The natural world is astounding. The swallows nesting now in the UK have flown 5,000 miles from Southern Africa earlier in the spring and will fly 5,000 miles back again in the autumn. They will do this every year for many years. Unbelievable.

'Is anything too hard for the Lord?' God had asked Abraham at the start of the Old Testament story (Genesis 18:14, NIV). And at the start of the New Testament story, the angel tells Mary that nothing God says is impossible. Though a virgin, she will have a son, and he will be the Son of God. Mary's cousin Elizabeth, despite being past the age of childbearing, is also expecting an 'impossible' baby in God's providence. We know too that the Lord Jesus did many 'impossible' things, and God raised him from the dead.

Mary believed that God was able to work things supernaturally far beyond her imagining. The apostle Paul believed it too when he wrote that God is able to 'accomplish abundantly far more than all we can ask or imagine' (Ephesians 3:20). We too can believe it. God can do things that human beings can't.

■ PRAYER

Lord, your ways are not our ways. Like Mary, may we be people with whom you can work wonders for our troubled world. Amen

Psalm 37:1a, 3–6a (NRSV)

Faith for all occasions

Do not fret because of the wicked... Trust in the Lord and do good; live in the land and enjoy security. Take delight in the Lord, and he will give you the desires of your heart. Commit your way to the Lord; trust in him, and he will act. He will make your vindication shine like the light.

What a difference a smart phone makes in all sorts of situations. It has maps and directions to save us getting lost; it updates us on the weather and the news; it enables us to send and receive texts and emails, to find out the times of buses and trains, to listen to music or to ring loved ones or emergency services. And we need never be bored in a waiting room again.

Faith, too, makes a big difference, whatever our situation. Putting our faith in Christ is the way into salvation and finding forgiveness and new life. Trusting in the Lord is key when living with difficulty or disappointment. Are you anxious about wicked people in positions of power? The Lord God is more active and powerful than they are, and he will outlast them. 'Commit your way to the Lord,' says the psalm, which is always a good move, but especially if we are vulnerable or facing a challenge.

■ PRAYER

Lord, in the time of temptation, in the hour of difficulty, in the day of sorrow, help me to have complete faith in you. Amen*

* A prayer by John Eddison

Mark 10:49b–52 (NIV)

An example of faith

So they called to the blind man, 'Cheer up! On your feet! He's calling you.' Throwing his cloak aside, he jumped to his feet and came to Jesus. 'What do you want me to do for you?' Jesus asked him. The blind man said, 'Rabbi, I want to see.' 'Go,' said Jesus, 'your faith has healed you.' Immediately he received his sight and followed Jesus along the road.

Bartimaeus was blind, begging from the passing crowds. When Jesus told him, 'Your faith has healed you' or, as in the NRSV, 'Your faith made you well,' immediately he could see. What did 'faith' involve for Bartimaeus?

Earlier in the incident, we read that Bartimaeus called out to Jesus for help, and he persisted in calling when people tried to deter him. Then he came to Jesus, and he was made well. Of course, it was the Lord Jesus who healed him. But his coming to Jesus had made it possible. Afterwards, Bartimaeus followed Jesus along the road, leaving his old life behind. Passers-by used to toss coins on to his cloak. He left that behind as well.

'Faith' is a comprehensive word in the New Testament. It 'covers a wide area of human trust and trustworthiness, merging into love at one end of the scale to loyalty at the other.'* Christian faith will involve for us, at different times, calling out to Christ, coming to him, loving him, recognising him, being loyal to him and following him along the road.

■ PRAYER

Pray for those with eye disease and sight loss, and those treating them and caring for them.

* Tom Wright, *Mark for Everyone* (SPCK, 2001), p. 230.

Matthew 17:20 (NIV, abridged)

Small faith, big outcome

[Jesus] replied... 'Truly I tell you, if you have faith as small as a mustard seed, you can say to this mountain, "Move from here to there," and it will move.'

I noticed a small boy standing at a bus stop with his mum. A bus approached, and the boy stepped forward and put out his hand. The bus stopped, and they got on. Faith works a bit like that. What made this multi-horsepower bus come to a stop? Not the strength of the boy's arm. It was the strength of the bus company's commitment to pick up passengers. The boy assumed it and acted on it. He was trusting it and it worked.

Jesus was speaking to his disciples along the same lines. His disciples should not get discouraged because they were lacking in faith. We should not get hung up on how strong or weak our faith is. What matters most is the strength of the thing in which we put our faith.

Elsewhere Jesus said, 'Have faith in God' (Mark 11:22). God's commitment to us is infinitely strong. Here Jesus uses memorable metaphors about a grain of seed and a high mountain to impress on us that just a speck of faith, putting out our hand to God's great faithfulness, can have big outcomes in proportion to our small faith.

■ PRAYER

Lord, when there are mountainous obstacles in my path, please remove them by your working, or show me how to negotiate them. Amen

Romans 4:3a, 20–21 (NRSV)

Abraham's faith

For what does scripture say? 'Abraham believed God'... No distrust made him waver concerning the promise of God, but he grew strong in his faith as he gave glory to God, being fully convinced that God was able to do what he had promised.

The promise of a pension accompanied many of us through our working lives. Then, following our retirement, a pension payment drops into our bank account every month. The Church of England Pensions Board is one of my favourite charities.

For years, Abraham's life was undergirded by God's big promises to bless him mightily. He and Sarah, though childless, would have a son. God promised him land that his descendants would possess; they would be a great nation, and beyond counting. God would bless the world through Abraham's offspring (Genesis 12:1–3).

Abraham was sometimes heroic, and sometimes he messed up. But he clung on to God's promises, through all the ups and downs. The Bible is the story of how these promises of God were fulfilled. It sees Abraham as the father of all who believe.

We too are beneficiaries of these promises from God, especially the gift of Christ, who himself made many promises for our lives. Not one will fail. The Lord will do what he has said.

■ PRAYER

Thank you, Lord, for your faithfulness and your 'precious and very great promises' (2 Peter 1:4). Keep me trusting you day by day. Amen

Romans 10:12b, 14, 17 (NRSV)

How does faith come?

The same Lord is Lord of all and is generous to all who call upon him... But how are they to call on one in whom they have not believed? And how are they to believe in one of whom they have never heard? And how are they to hear without someone to proclaim him?... So faith comes from what is heard, and what is heard comes through the word of Christ.

How do we come to have faith in a doctor? Through what she says and does. Similarly, how can we get faith in Christ? Through his words and deeds. A man was walking into Damascus one day when he heard his name being called: 'Saul, Saul.' It was the voice of the risen Christ on this, the first day of Saul's Christian faith. Paul (as Saul was to become) was speaking from experience when he wrote that faith comes from hearing the word of Christ.

It was probably so for our own faith too. Words of Christ, or words about Christ, may have reached us from the cradle or Sunday school; or through exposure to the Bible or church worship; or through Christian friends or a gospel speaker. Somehow, the Lord got through to us, and we 'heard'.

Our faith will get stronger as we meditate on what the Bible says about Jesus and what he did. And his words have never been equalled. Let them sustain you day by day.

■ **PRAYER**

Lord, encourage and strengthen all those seeking to bring the message of Christ to others. Amen

John 11:25–27 (NRSV)

Believe in me

Jesus said to [Martha], 'I am the resurrection and the life. Those who believe in me, even though they die, will live, and everyone who lives and believes in me will never die. Do you believe this?' She said to him, 'Yes, Lord, I believe that you are the Messiah, the Son of God, the one coming into the world.'

Martha is deeply upset. Her brother was taken ill three days ago. They sent for Jesus but he did not come straightaway as they expected. Now Jesus comes, but he is too late. Her brother has already died.

Poor Martha. Do you think of her as a busy hostess, bustling around, hard-working and careworn? One might think so from Luke's gospel (10:38–42). But here we see her as a thoughtful believer. In her grief, she articulates a confession of faith as great as anyone else in the New Testament: 'Yes, Lord, I believe that you are the Messiah, the Son of God, the one coming into the world.'

Where will Martha find comfort in her loss? In the future resurrection? Maybe. But better than that, Jesus draws her to himself, there and then. The resurrection life is standing right in front of her. 'I am it!' is his message. 'I will never let you down, even in death. Do you believe this? Believe in me.'

■ PRAYER

Pray for those who come alongside the bereaved and the dying, that they may bring companionship, support and hope for the future.

Romans 5:1–2 (NIV)

Free access

Therefore, since we have been justified through faith, we have peace with God through our Lord Jesus Christ, through whom we have gained access by faith into this grace in which we now stand. And we boast in the hope of the glory of God.

It was an absorbing Wimbledon final. There were two young children watching from the front row, clearly enjoying the tennis and the whole occasion. Photos of them went round the world. The Princess of Wales, patron of the All England Lawn Tennis and Croquet Club in Wimbledon, was introducing her two eldest children, George and Charlotte, to the event. They met players and other guests, and no doubt they enjoyed the strawberries too.

Our Lord Jesus Christ is our introduction into the world not of tennis, but of 'this grace', says Paul here in Romans. Christ brings us into a whole new world, the 'sphere of God's grace' (NEB), where his goodness and mercy hold sway. Christ has called us to accompany him into God's presence, and we now enjoy peace with God and all other blessings that come through the Lord Jesus. This is our standing, which he has secured for us and now is ours to thrive in.

Christ brings us to God. He is our access, our introduction. Our part – having faith – is to take his hand as he ushers us into his Father's presence.

■ PRAYER

Pray for any you know who feel rejected or isolated in the world. Lord Jesus Christ, grant them to know your peace and the warmth of your welcome. Amen

John 7:37–39a (NIV)

Outward-flowing faith

On the last and greatest day of the festival, Jesus stood and said in a loud voice, 'Let anyone who is thirsty come to me and drink. Whoever believes in me, as Scripture has said, rivers of living water will flow from within them.' By this he meant the Spirit, whom those who believed in him were later to receive.

When we knock over a glass, or a river breaks its banks, the water spreads out as much as it can. After a dry spell, we welcome the rain running along gullies and furrows, reviving the plants and swelling the fruit.

Jesus was in Jerusalem, and it was festival time, a festival at which they prayed for rain for the harvest. The festival included a daily ceremony of pouring out water in the temple. On the final day of the festival, Jesus announced loudly that anyone who believed in him would have rivers of living water flowing out from their innermost being.

The message was that when we come to Jesus and drink of his blessings, not only shall we know deep satisfaction ourselves, but blessings will also flow out from us to others. This is what the Spirit of Jesus does in a believer. The world does not know how much it owes to the Spirit's work in believers and to their Christian character, prayers, witness and service flowing into the world.

■ PRAYER

Lord Jesus, may the faith of my heart translate into benefit and blessing to others. Amen

Hebrews 11:7–34 (NRSV, abridged)

People of faith

By faith Noah... built an ark... By faith Abraham obeyed... as did Isaac and Jacob... By faith Moses... By faith the people passed through the Red Sea... Time would fail me to tell of Gideon, Barak, Samson, Jephthah, of David and Samuel and the prophets, who through faith conquered kingdoms, administered justice, obtained promises.

A clergyman friend of mine was taking a funeral in Israel, and he read a section of Hebrews 11 in the service. A rabbi who was present was so moved by the stirring words that he asked for a copy, unaware that the words came from the New Testament.

This famous chapter (Hebrews 11) is like a National Portrait Gallery of Jewish heroes of faith. We recognise obvious characters like Abraham, but there are less obvious ones too. We see Sarah, Joseph, Moses' mother and father, Rahab a prostitute, Elijah, Daniel and others. They all trusted God. The story of God in the Old Testament came about through people who bravely believed him, obeyed him and followed him into a future they could not see.

There is a room in this gallery for our portraits too. Those believers pressed on to what God was calling them to, and we too press on to the promised future to which Christ is calling us.

■ PRAYER

Lord, thank you for these Old Testament people. May my faith be as resilient and as resolute as theirs. Amen

The Gift of Years

 Debbie Thrower is the pioneer of BRF Ministries' Anna Chaplaincy for Older People ministry, offering spiritual care to older people, and is widely involved in training and advocacy.

Visit **annachaplaincy.org.uk** to find out more.

Debbie writes...

Welcome!

In this issue, I am drawn to all that Lynn Goslin has discovered about Jesus' approach to people. He is the consummate listener. We can learn much from his example; 'What do you want me to do for you?' is his oft-repeated question. Jesus knows how to reach into the heart of our concerns. When I first came across Abraham Schmitt's words, I knew I wanted to share them in the *Anna Chaplaincy Handbook*. They are useful pointers for all of us in our different relationships:

'Listening with love transforms what it loves… To listen totally means that one takes another's whole life into one's being and cares for it… People intuitively measure the depth of love of all persons in all interpersonal relationships. If love is felt to be genuine, they will reveal much. If it is lacking, they will then say nothing important… Listening on this level is a creative art. It means that the fragmented pieces of a person are brought together into a single meaningful whole. A new life is born at that moment.'*

I hope this edition of reflections conveys to you the peace and joy of Christ's love.

Debbie

* Abraham Schmitt, *The Art of Listening with Love* (Abingdon Press, 1982)

Prophetic women

Lynn Goslin wrote about conversations certain New Testament men and women had with Jesus. She showed how Jesus listened deeply to what was said – or not said – and got to the truth of every character and every situation. The prophets of the Old Testament model a different kind of conversation with God: listening to what God wanted to say and delivering God's message, however challenging or unwelcome. In this extract from Clare and Micah Hayns' *Unveiled: Women of the Old Testament and the choices they made*, we read Huldah's story.

The Hebrew word for prophet is *nabi* (male) or *nebiah* (female), which comes from *naba*, meaning 'call'. We are far more familiar with the male *nabi* in the Old Testament, such as Moses, Isaiah and Jeremiah. Although there are only a few prophetic women mentioned in the Hebrew scriptures, the text doesn't indicate they were particularly unusual, so there may well have been others whose stories haven't survived. Miriam, Deborah and Huldah have very different gifts, but they reveal that God has been speaking through women for many centuries.

There are occasions in life when we receive news that we don't want to hear, news that we know will change our lives from that moment on: a diagnosis of a terminal illness, the death of a loved one, a global pandemic. When King Josiah was handed a long-lost manuscript that had been unearthed from the ruins of the temple, he knew that his life, and the life of all his people, was about to be transformed. It was bad news. Huldah was the prophetess who was called upon to impart just how bad this news was to be.

Huldah was a woman from Judah who lived in Jerusalem with her husband Shallum. He was 'keeper of the wardrobe', a job which probably involved looking after the robes of the priests, rather like a verger would in our churches today. They lived during the turbulent times of a seemingly endless cycle of corrupt and cruel kings ruling the divided nations of Israel and Judah. During this period the temple in Jerusalem had been allowed to fall into ruin, the people had turned again to idolatry, and the laws and statutes given to Moses had largely been forgotten.

Josiah was one of the few kings who 'did what was right in the sight of the Lord' (2 Kings 22:2, NRSV), ruling with justice and equity, ensuring those who worked on the restoration of the temple were paid, and that all the temple funds were accounted for properly. Yet all this was not enough to prevent the catastrophe that was to come.

When the king heard the words from the rediscovered 'book of the law' (the book of Deuteronomy) read to him, he realised with remorse how far his people had turned from God's will. He wanted to understand more and, as Huldah was clearly well known in the community as a prophet, his priests sent for her to help interpret what they were reading. Huldah spoke with authority, clarity and boldness, and did not hide the gravity of what God was saying to them, that Judah would soon be destroyed: 'Because they have abandoned me and have made offerings to other gods, so that they have provoked me to anger with all the work of their hands, therefore my wrath will be kindled against this place, and it will not be quenched' (2 Kings 22:17, NRSV).

The only good news for Josiah was that, because of his repentance, humility and remorse, the inevitable destruction would be delayed until after his death. Huldah's prophetic words came to pass, and soon after Josiah died the kingdom of Judah was decimated by two Babylonian invasions. By the end of the book of Kings, the once-glorious rule of David and Solomon was in ruins. The king (Jehoiachin) was imprisoned; the priests, leaders and craftsmen were exiled; the temple and city walls were destroyed; and even the remaining treasures of Solomon's splendid era were melted down.

There wouldn't be another king in Judah until a very different king came along, also from David's lineage. This king was born into poverty and was led to his death with a crown of thorns on his head, and his resurrection would be the ultimate good news for all people.

Not many people relish the role of 'prophet of doom', and it takes great courage. Huldah joins the other great prophets of the Bible, such as Jonah, Daniel and Micah, who tell the truth even though their message is hard to hear.

When we hear really bad news, often there is not much we can do about the situation itself – a loved one remains sick, a conflict continues… But we do have a choice as to how we respond to it. Josiah chose to respond to Huldah's words by falling to his knees in prayer and following God 'with all his heart and all his soul' (2 Kings 23:3, NRSV). Perhaps that is a good place to start.

Unveiled
Women of the Old Testament and the choices they made
Clare Hayns and Micah Hayns
978 1 80039 072 0   £14.99
brfonline.org.uk

Zacchaeus

The poet Ann Lewin is perhaps best known for her much-loved collection of poems and prayers, *Watching for the Kingfisher*. Her moving poem 'Zacchaeus', from that collection, is the perfect complement to Lynn Goslin's reflection 'Trying to see' on page 9.

I walk tall now.
After those years of
Having to make my mark
Fair means or foul,
I know myself valued.
Elbowed out of the way,
Forced to assert myself
The only way I knew,
By getting rich at your
Expense, even having to
Climb a tree because
You wouldn't let me see…

And then, he saw me,
Looked and saw me,
Scared that my littleness
Would keep me down.
He looked and said,
'It's you I want,
Come down and let me
Join you at your house.'

Me!

And now, I'll never be the same again.
From now on I can look you in the eye.
I'll give back all I too unfairly,
What's more, I'll give it back four-fold.
And all because he looked at me and
Saw me, and loved me as I was and
As I am.

I walk tall now.

The poet Ann Lewin was a teacher of RE and English for 27 years and has written a number of times for *Bible Reflections for Older People*. Now retired, she writes, leads quiet days and retreats and works with individuals and groups, helping people explore their spirituality. She has had experience of caring for people living with dementia, first her mother and then one of her brothers, over a period of about 35 years.

Emlyn Williams meets *Bible Reflections for Older People* readers in Norfolk

When *Bible Reflections for Older People* writer Emlyn Williams moved recently to a Norfolk village, 40 years after he first worked in the area, little did he expect to meet one of his former colleagues the first time he and his wife 'Tricia, another of our treasured writers, went to their new village church. But that's what happened. There was Carolyn. According to Emlyn, 'it's been a totally unexpected renewal of friendship after all these years.' But there was more: 'The really intriguing thing is that Carolyn faithfully runs a little Bible study group in North Pickenham and it turns out that they've been reading *Bible Reflections for Older People*'. Carolyn invited him along to meet the group and see what they do. 'She said I might learn something, and the group might learn something from me about writing for *Bible Reflections for Older People*.'

That meeting took place just as Emlyn was putting the finishing touches to his series on peace and joy for this issue. 'It's a lovely group of elderly ladies,' he reports, 'and it was really striking that the one who is the oldest, at 91, is still very active and involved. She used to be the receptionist at the local doctor's surgery. She retired 35 years ago but she's still going strong and is a bit of a leading light within the group.'

Emlyn found 'a straightforward, traditional Bible study group'. They all had a copy of the booklet and they'd read the verse and the reflection and then somebody would lead a little bit of a discussion about it. 'And there was cake at the end: it's very Norfolk to have cake! And it was lovely really to see them wanting to get together to talk and learn and pray. It was very simple, but that kind of simplicity is sometimes deceptive: it can actually take you quite deep.'

And that is what Emlyn enjoys most about writing for *Bible Reflections for Older People*. 'It's very different from writing Scripture Union notes, which are much more focused on unpacking Bible texts. With *Bible Reflections for Older People* there's more freedom to explore themes: sometimes a series starts with a few random thoughts and a lot of Googling, but gradually something comes together and it's amazing to see how that happens and what eventually emerges.'

The other thing that never ceases to amaze both Emlyn and 'Tricia is how notes that were written perhaps 12, even 18 months earlier, can be profoundly relevant on the day they're read, either for an individual in particular circumstances, or for everyone in the face of some kind of national or international crisis.

'When that happens,' says Emlyn, 'it's absolutely spine-tingling. There's no way that you could know what's going to be happening so far ahead: you just have to trust God to make it be what it needs to be for people.'

What does he hope that readers take away from his latest series of reflections? 'I'd like people to take away that God really does want them to know his joy and peace. These are people who will be going through a range of circumstances, and maybe facing a not very joyful or peaceful future in one sense. So I hope that there's some comfort for people in this series, but not just comfort. I hope I'm pointing them to where true comfort might come from.'

Carolyn Vincent, Emlyn's friend and former colleague who introduced her Bible study group to *Bible Reflections for Older People*.

Within the waves
Clare O'Driscoll

I have something of a reputation among my friends for being mildly obsessed with the sea. It's not just the blustery walks, salty air breeze and invigorating all-weather swims, but also because the sea speaks to me of all the contradictions and complexities of life. There are gentle sunlit days, but also crashing stormy ones – and both have something to teach us.

I think particularly of a stay in Mexico when a cyclone struck overnight. The merry waves we had splashed in the previous evening had, within hours, become deadly, conspiring with the wind to reshape the beach's landscape into a clutter of deep ravines and fallen trees.

Like the sea, our lives and faith journeys can be both gentle and tumultuous, life-giving and even dangerous, sometimes changing overnight. At the beach, where squalling high-tide waves later soften into lapping shallows, we are aware of all these contradictions. It reminds us of our own limitations and complexities and how, in all this, God is with us. God is still God.

In the following reflections, we look at the sea's rhythms, how the waves change from lulling to wild and back again, and what we can learn there about our walk with God.

Jeremiah 5:22b (NIV)

The safe shore

'I made the sand a boundary for the sea, an everlasting barrier it cannot cross. The waves may roll, but they cannot prevail; they may roar, but they cannot cross it.'

One wild December afternoon on Brighton beach, I wandered down to the shoreline, standing a little way back for fear of the huge crashing waves. They were mighty, awe-inspiring and more than a little scary as they swelled high and broke in explosive, frothy arcs.

However, for all their noise and grandeur, by the time the water reached where I stood, they were no more than a gently foaming fizz. Nothing to worry about after all.

Threatening 'waves' of trouble in life can look overwhelming as they rage and curl to their peak, but often, by the time they reach us, they have run their course. In between their early frightening immensity and the soft splash at the shore, God is at work, bigger than all of it and in the business of calming storms. He sets a boundary around us so that, even if those waves are there, they become a gently foaming fizz in his presence. And while the sand may seem a strange boundary to contain an angry sea, God is never limited by weakness. In his presence, huge waves soften on the shore.

■ PRAYER

Thank you, Father God, that you know everything that's ahead. You see the waves of trouble that threaten to overwhelm and you place a boundary around us. Amen

Micah 7:19 (NIV)

A clean start

You will again have compassion on us; you will tread our sins underfoot and hurl all our iniquities into the depths of the sea.

The Atlantic crashed on our left as we drove along the deserted early morning road. We parked up next to the beach and smiled. The previous day we had seen it dotted with tourists and clutter but now, at 7.00 am, we had the wide expanse of sand to ourselves. And what sand it was – still wet from the tide, velvet smooth and gleaming like an ice rink.

Any imperfections from the day before were hard to even imagine in the golden dawn, all forgotten in the light of the smooth perfection of a beach just washed clean. Later, life would inevitably happen: broken sandcastles, footprints, perhaps a dent where someone stumbles, splodges of dropped ice cream and left-behind picnic scraps.

However, every night all the debris and disorder is hurled back into the depths of the ocean. By morning, all that remains is the peaceful sight of freshly washed sand. Similarly, when we turn to God, all our imperfections and mess are gathered back into the depths of his love. Whatever marks in the sand we have made, we can be confident that in Christ, God's mercies return every morning, with powerful waves of forgiveness, bringing peace and washing us clean.

■ **PRAYER**

Thank you, Jesus, for your endless compassion and forgiving love for us despite our imperfections and daily stumbles. Amen

Matthew 14:29b (NIV)

Peninsulas not islands

Then Peter got down out of the boat, walked on the water and came towards Jesus.

We hung around nervously by the tiny bobbing ferry – just big enough for a handful of people plus supplies for the island. It was debatable whether it would go. More worrying, however, was whether the wind would allow the return ferry to bring us back. There is something magical about visiting an island, but there's also a sense of dependency. You cannot just leave. You have, literally, cut off your connections.

When we look at Jesus, we see he valued solitude but always stayed connected with God and others. After taking time out to pray, he went to find his friends, even walking on water to reach them.

We probably won't walk on water but perhaps we can be like peninsulas, keeping open pathways to God and others. Fittingly, the French word for peninsula is *presqu'île* – an 'almost-island'. We can have island seclusion without cutting everything off, and we can find peace without isolating ourselves completely. Perhaps a 'spiritual peninsula' would be solitude in God's presence.

We need time apart, but we also need relationship, both with God and within Christian communities. While Peter's next steps may have faltered, his example of walking towards Jesus is one we can always follow.

■ **PRAYER**

Compassionate Christ, help us to follow your example in connecting with others and, when we long for solitude, may we find it in your presence. Amen

Habakkuk 2:14 (NIV)

Ripples

For the earth shall be filled with the knowledge of the glory of the Lord as the waters cover the sea.

The waves at Inchydoney Beach were wide and shallow – a morning of hazy sea mist and rain-speckled sand. We walked around the dunes and found a lake of seawater the tides had left behind. My husband and son – the pebble skimmers of our family – gathered a pile of flat stones and got down to business. Never having mastered the skill myself, I was content to watch the pebbles bounce across the water, gazing at the mesmerising patterns of circles spiralling outwards.

Some of the ripples were wide, endlessly circling, bumping into each other like gentle dodgems. Then there were smaller circles of raindrops dancing on the water's surface, mingling with the larger ones.

Our lives and our loves are like ripples, bumping into others, overlapping and spreading. When we let God's Spirit fill us and guide us, those ripples will flow grace over all the connections we make. Sometimes our ripples are big, making an obvious difference to the world. Sometimes they are less grandiose, perhaps simply a kind word or gesture. Even when our ripples seem small to us, how we live our lives shows Jesus to others and spreads the knowledge of God's glory.

■ **PRAYER**

Holy Spirit, may the love you have placed in us ripple out to the world, bouncing into others with life-changing grace. Amen

Psalm 139:9–10 (NIV)

Meeting the dawn

If I rise on the wings of the dawn, if I settle on the far side of the sea, even there your hand will guide me, your right hand will hold me fast.

The clock read 5.50 am. I'd jolted awake for no reason. I could try to sleep more or… if I threw on clothes and ran, I might make sunrise on the beach, five minutes away from our holiday let. There wasn't time for an internal struggle, but I had one anyway. Would it even be a good sunrise? It could be cloudy. Bed was warm and comfy – there was no guarantee it was worth leaving.

The sunrise won by a tiny margin. I scuttled past the lighthouse and gazed across the sea through the milky dawn. Within minutes, the sun edged up into a cloudless sky, resplendent and breathtaking, painting long-legged shadows of the pier on to tangerine sands. I couldn't stop smiling. I'd made the right choice.

Obviously, this was an inconsequential decision, but sometimes God draws us to a new challenge – a big move or a simple act of kindness. We know it's good but it is still hard to leave our comfort zone and trust it will be worth stepping out. Yet when we struggle with fear and decisions, we can know that wherever we go, whatever we do, God is there, holding us.

■ **PRAYER**
Thank you, God, for guiding us in our decisions, big and small, and for holding us wherever we go. Amen

Isaiah 49:10b (NIV)

Lost in the tides

He who has compassion on them will guide them and lead them by springs of water.

It was the most incredible proposal ever. We gazed down at the artists as they worked on the giant image, carving champagne bubbles into the sand alongside the words 'Will you marry me?' It must have taken hours.

Eventually we had to leave and didn't witness the actual question being popped. I felt a little sad that, being drawn on tide-washed sand, it would completely disappear within a day. All that work. All that art and beauty and time – gone. And yet, the love behind the gesture, the excitement of the moment: those will never be forgotten.

When a fruitful season ends, it can feel like the waves have carried something precious away. When you step back from life-defining work or are no longer able to do something significant, it can feel like that part of you is gone forever, lost to the tides of time.

Yet our God of compassion does not forget. God sees your whole life, remembers your past goodness and still leads you towards new things. Just when it feels like all that is precious has been washed away, God does a new thing, leading you to fresh springs of water.

■ PRAYER

When I feel like a part of me has been lost, guide me, Father, to the new springs of water you have prepared for me. Amen

Ephesians 4:14a (NIV)

The wisdom of groynes

Then we will no longer be infants, tossed back and forth by the waves, and blown here and there by every wind of teaching.

They were impressive. The biggest beach groynes I'd ever seen, standing tall, sharp-edged and blocky in newly cut wood, pointing to the sky and shouting their strength. The older ones further up the beach had diminished into smooth stumps, like dot-shaped sculptures moulded by the tides. Then I noticed something. The new groynes had been placed next to older ones, as though leaning on them, girdled together. However strong and impressive the new ones were, they needed to be anchored in ancient wisdom. They needed the older ones to show them where to stand, how to do this thing.

As the years pass, we can sometimes feel diminished, but Jesus valued everyone from the tiniest child to the elderly and infirm. He gave importance to everyone, no matter what their age or background. Through the older generation, God shows the 'new ones' how to stand. There is wisdom and experience there, a steadfastness that remains firm through all the changing winds of time.

The 'new' can sometimes seem better and shinier – and certainly does have a lot to offer – but there is both beauty and wisdom in age, signposts for the next generation and a vivid example of God's enduring presence.

■ **PRAYER**

Whatever stage of life we are at, help us, Lord, to share our strengths and learn from those of others. Amen

2 Samuel 22:16a (NIV)

What is hidden

The valleys of the sea were exposed and the foundations of the earth laid bare.

The tide was so low it looked like someone had pulled the plug out, exposing the seabed in all its natural messiness, hidden things revealed. Some beaches boast smooth sand at low tide, but this one was all rock pools, seaweed and driftwood.

The tide comes back in – always – but there is value in the laying bare too. All that has been hidden is seen. There is mess, but also beauty and texture in that uncovering. The egrets stalk around, lazily dipping their beaks for food. It is less 'beach in Sunday best' and more 'just out of bed', real and gritty. We see its scars. When the time is right, the waves roll back in, first gently, taking care of those hidden places, then with power, washing everything clean.

The thought of being exposed can be frightening but, just as low tide reveals treasures in the bones of the beach, we too can be seen as we are. Jesus sees all that is hidden under our 'tides' and loves us completely. And then, as with the beach exposed at low tide, his holy waves of peace and healing roll in, first gently, taking care of those hidden things, then with power, washing everything clean.

■ **PRAYER**

Jesus, when we would rather cover up our hearts, let us trust you to find beauty in our hidden places. Amen

John 7:38 (NIV)

Overflowing joy

'Whoever believes in me, as Scripture has said, rivers of living water will flow from within them.'

The weather had turned. A cartoon-like puff of purple cloud hung over the sea while colossal waves smashed on to the sand. Suddenly, channels of clear water flooded up alongside the groynes – bubbling streams overflowing from the angry sea.

They gushed towards us, full of life, but, unlike the waves, they brought no fear. We'd been so focused on the wild sea we hadn't noticed them froth up by our feet. We giggled in surprise, caught off guard.

Life can hurl some storms at us but, within them, we can still be surprised by God's joy – overflowing and without measure. That joy brings the strength to keep going. When we believe in Christ, the tumultuous sea will still be there, but alongside it will be rivers of living water. Within our struggles and sorrows, God of the unexpected can bring blessings.

Of course, God does not plan storms for us, but when they come, he can make them work for good, like joyful streams flowing up the beach when all we could see was the raging waves. When it feels like we might sink, God gives us the joyful splash and hope of life.

■ **PRAYER**

Thank you, Father, that when waves of difficulty come crashing in, you temper them with streams of living water, giving us joy, strength and clarity to keep going. Amen

Isaiah 44:3a (NIV)

The tide comes in

For I will pour water on the thirsty land, and streams on the dry ground.

I had waited so long for this – to swim in the sea again after a cold winter and a too busy spring. It had become a longing, almost a physical thirst. Now, finally I was here, and I'd somehow misjudged the tides. There was effectively nothing to swim in. Although I love splashing in shallows, there are times when you need more depth.

However ridiculous it sounds, my disappointment felt overwhelming that day, almost as if this thing would never happen. Yet a couple of weeks later I unexpectedly found myself back at the coast. This time the tide was high, the water deep and buoyant.

There are times when our faith feels a little shallow. There are times when we yearn for the fulfilment of a long-awaited hope, or simply for more depth. Such longing can have sharp edges. It's hard to keep waiting, and sometimes it feels like this thing will never happen. But, in time, those thin shallows will grow; high tide will come. When we feel parched, God is steadfast and faithful, giving us future hope, filling us with new life and taking us deeper into love.

Whatever we might be thirsting for, God knows. God's timing is perfect, and that tide will come back in.

■ **PRAYER**
Faithful God, thank you that your promises are true and your tides of love will always come back in. Amen

Peace and joy

Emlyn Williams

In Hong Kong and Macau there is a chain of upmarket ladies' shoe shops called 'Joy & Peace'. In the UK, 'Joy & Peace Ltd' is the name of an estate agent, though I have to say I've never found the experience of buying and selling houses particularly joyful or peaceful. A quick internet search reveals that there are many other companies around the world using joy and peace in their name.

In the Bible, joy and peace are neither a shoe shop nor an estate agent. They are two of the nine characteristics of Christians that Paul calls the 'fruit of the Spirit' (Galatians 5:22–23, NIV). He puts these characteristics in direct contrast to a list of destructive and evil actions which he calls the 'acts of the flesh' (Galatians 5:19–21, NIV). One way to look at the fruit of the Spirit, including joy and peace, is to see them as a checklist for the way Christians should live and behave.

But while that may be helpful to an extent, it also misses the point. We don't work through them in sequence, ticking them off as we achieve them. Rather, we might see them as an overall picture of the kind of person God calls us to be. So, as we read these reflections, let's pray that God will help us to cooperate with him in producing the fruit of the Spirit in our lives.

Galatians 5:22–25 (NIV)

Wonderful fruit

But the fruit of the Spirit is love, joy, peace, forbearance, kindness, goodness, faithfulness, gentleness and self-control. Against such things there is no law. Those who belong to Christ Jesus have crucified the flesh with its passions and desires. Since we live by the Spirit, let us keep in step with the Spirit.

When we lived in Australia we had a grapefruit tree in our garden. To say that it was fruitful was a massive understatement. We did nothing to encourage it: no feeding, no pruning – it just sat there producing seemingly endless fruit. Unfortunately our friends and neighbours also had grapefruit trees so we literally couldn't give the fruit away. The lawn around that tree would be covered with fallen grapefruit, and I would take the easy way out and run the lawnmower over them. It looked a bit messy, but the scent was wonderful.

Joy and peace come to us from the Holy Spirit. Along with the other qualities in that list, Paul says that they are the fruit of the Spirit. Notice that he says 'fruit' not 'fruits' – we can't pick and choose between them. They aren't things which we can manufacture. They are a package. Our part in all this is to cooperate with the Spirit, to 'keep in step' with him.

■ **PRAYER**

Thank you, Father, that you are at work in me to produce the fruit which is impossible for me to produce myself. Help me today to keep in step with what you are doing in my life. Amen

Luke 2:10, 13–14 (NIV)

Joy and peace

But the angel said to them, 'Do not be afraid. I bring you good news that will cause great joy for all the people'... Suddenly a great company of the heavenly host appeared with the angel, praising God and saying, 'Glory to God in the highest heaven, and on earth peace to those on whom his favour rests.'

I'm often frustrated by how hard it is to find Christmas cards that reflect the Christmas story. Santa, snowmen, reindeer, cute animals of all kinds, holly and mistletoe, Christmas crackers and puddings, dubious jokes and cartoons – you can find them all very easily. I remember receiving one card which had an Australian crimson rosella bird sitting on a snowy eucalyptus tree branch. Very confusing.

Sadly, classic nativity scenes now seem to be rare on Christmas cards. However, one-word message cards: joy, peace and love – in any combination – are still there, and they get to the heart of the Christmas message. The angel announced to the shepherds news that would 'cause great joy for all the people'. The coming of Jesus changed things for everyone, not just for Jewish people. As for peace? The age-old hostility between humans and God created by our rebellion would come to an end.

■ **PRAYER**

Thank you, Father, that the joy and peace we often see on Christmas cards can be our experience every day. Help me to reflect that joy and peace to those I meet today. Amen

Luke 24:36, 40–41a (NIV, abridged)

Too good to be true?

While they were still talking about this, Jesus himself stood among them and said to them, 'Peace be with you'… When he had said this, he showed them his hands and feet… they still did not believe it because of joy and amazement.

One day I woke up with an earworm, a tune that just wouldn't go away. I was under great stress and very anxious about things at work. Going round in my head was an old song from a record which my parents used to play, 'He whispered "Peace be still"'. Amazingly, as I lay in bed that morning, those words brought me the peace that I so desperately needed. Have you ever had a similar experience?

When Jesus appeared to his disciples after his resurrection and said, 'Peace be with you,' they didn't believe it. Some good news is just too good to be true and it takes time to sink in. I wonder what might stop you believing Jesus' promise of peace. Fear? Past experience? Lack of faith? The good thing is that Jesus was patient with the disciples. He didn't just show them his hands and feet; he let them touch them. He wanted them to believe in the peace he brought, and he wants us to believe in it too.

■ **PRAYER**

Are you finding it difficult to experience the peace which Jesus promised? Picture yourself in the scene with the disciples as he says, 'Peace be with you.' Take time sitting in his presence and receive his peace.

Romans 15:13 (NIV)

Overflowing hope

May the God of hope fill you with all joy and peace as you trust in him, so that you may overflow with hope by the power of the Holy Spirit.

I've always struggled to know when to end a letter or an email with 'Yours sincerely' or 'Yours faithfully'. Perhaps that's why some people use 'Kind regards' or something similar as a sign off or valediction. Today's verse is an example of how Paul did it, although he used at least two more variations (15:33; 16:25–27) before he finally finished. It's what some people call a 'prayer-wish'. Think of one of your friends or family. What would you wish for them today?

Joy and peace are great things to wish and pray for people – you can't go wrong, can you? But it can sound a bit vague and be no more than wishful thinking. Paul took the Christians to whom he was writing back to the source of true joy and peace: the God of hope. The way to receive God's joy and peace, Paul says, is simply to trust God; to focus on him and not the things that are going on around us. The outcome is an overflowing of deep joy and peace.

■ **PRAYER**

Help me today, Father, to trust you, whatever is happening. Let me be filled with joy, peace and hope that will overflow to those around me. Amen

Nehemiah 8:10 (NIV)

Joyful celebration

Nehemiah said, 'Go and enjoy choice food and sweet drinks, and send some to those who have nothing prepared. This day is holy to our Lord. Do not grieve, for the joy of the Lord is your strength.'

Food, drink and joyful celebration may not fit too well with our idea of a solemn holy day. Grieving may seem more appropriate. This marathon reading of the Book of the Law (8:3), which had been lost for such a long time then rediscovered, caused the people to weep. They realised that they had neglected it, so perhaps it's surprising that Nehemiah prescribes a celebration. But the day was holy because it was a reminder of what God had done for his people: of course it should lead to rejoicing.

There are two important lessons here. First, the law wasn't simply read to the people: the Levites explained it to them so that they understood. And because they understood, they were able to celebrate (v. 12). Second, their joy was to spill over to other people. They were to send some of the special food and drink 'to those who have nothing pre- pared'. God had been generous to them, and they were to be generous to others. Joy is something to spread around.

■ PRAYER

Thank you, Father, for all that you have done for me. Help me to rejoice in your kindness and generosity. May that joy spill over to the people I meet today. Amen

John 14:26–27 (NIV)

Real peace

'But the Advocate, the Holy Spirit, whom the Father will send in my name, will teach you all things and will remind you of everything I have said to you. Peace I leave with you; my peace I give you. I do not give to you as the world gives. Do not let your hearts be troubled and do not be afraid.'

Thirty-five years ago some family and friends came to Gatwick Airport to say goodbye as we left for Australia. None of us knew when we would see each other again. The excitement of going to a new country was mixed with sadness as we realised what that might mean. So imagine what it was like for the disciples as Jesus prepared them for the reality that he would be leaving them.

Jesus promised two things. First, the Father would send someone to them who would be a constant presence. On earth, Jesus could be in only one place at a time. But the Holy Spirit would continue to teach them. He would remind them of everything Jesus had taught them. They would be better off than when Jesus was present. And Jesus also promised them his peace: peace of a completely different quality to anything else. Paul would later say that it 'exceeds anything we can understand' (Philippians 4:7, NLT). Real peace.

■ PRAYER
Thank you, Father, for the Holy Spirit's constant presence. Help me today to listen to his voice as he continues to teach me, reminding me of what Jesus said. Amen

Philippians 4:4–7 (NIV)

Easier said than done

Rejoice in the Lord always. I will say it again: rejoice! Let your gentleness be evident to all. The Lord is near. Do not be anxious about anything, but in every situation, by prayer and petition, with thanksgiving, present your requests to God. And the peace of God, which transcends all understanding, will guard your hearts and your minds in Christ Jesus.

Being told to cheer up can be so irritating. Paul repeats his command to rejoice, and he had already said it in the previous chapter as well (3:1). It must have been important. If we think of rejoicing as a feeling, an emotion, it's not surprising that it can be so difficult. But here Paul is talking about rejoicing as an action, something we can choose to do. Perhaps recognising the nearness of God makes it easier.

Paul's recipe for dealing with anxiety has four ingredients: prayer, petition, thanksgiving and requests. Thanksgiving, in particular, focuses our mind on what God has done in the past. The old hymn 'Count your blessings' says that if you do that, it will 'surprise you what the Lord has done'. So prayer can open the way to God's peace in our lives. That peace 'is far more wonderful than the human mind can understand' (v. 7, TLB) and it can act as a sentry to our hearts and minds, guarding us from being overwhelmed by fear and anxiety.

■ PRAYER
Try to recall ways in which God has protected you in the past. Bring your present concerns to him and ask for his peace.

Romans 5:1–2a (NIV)

Peace with God

Therefore, since we have been justified through faith, we have peace with God through our Lord Jesus Christ, through whom we have gained access by faith into this grace in which we now stand.

There's an old hymn which I don't often hear these days, with a verse which says, 'Peace, perfect peace, with loved ones far away? In Jesus' keeping we are safe, and they.' I remember a preacher pointing out – with a twinkle in his eye – that you can interpret that first line in two ways. Don't we all like a bit of peace and quiet?

But peace is not just a feeling of tranquillity or quiet, what happens when you put your feet up after a busy day. Paul spoke about that on another occasion (Philippians 4:7). Here he is talking about peace with God. Our sin had separated us from God, but now through faith in Jesus we have been put right with God, justified ('just as if I'd never sinned'). The barrier between us has been removed, and so through Jesus we have peace with God. One writer says, 'Paul means that the believer is always on God's side.' Isn't it great that peace with God leads us to the peace of God?

■ **PRAYER**

Take a few moments to think about what peace with God means to you. As you sit in his presence, thank him for putting right what was wrong, making peace with God possible for you.

Romans 14:16–18 (NIV)

Pursue peace and joy

Therefore do not let what you know is good be spoken of as evil. For the kingdom of God is not a matter of eating and drinking, but of righteousness, peace and joy in the Holy Spirit, because anyone who serves Christ in this way is pleasing to God and receives human approval.

Christians are not exempt from arguing – far from it. And sometimes we argue about the strangest things. Food, drink, clothes, entertainment – all of them have at times been a source of great conflict. Often this has led to new denominations starting. I heard of one church whose main distinctive feature was that they didn't believe in keeping dogs, on the basis of Philippians 3:2, 'Watch out for those dogs.'

The Christians in Rome disagreed about the significance of certain days (sabbath, festivals, v. 5), diet (meat or vegetables, v. 2) and probably other things as well because they were from different cultures, Jewish and Gentile. The real problem wasn't that they had different points of view but that they were judging one another (vv. 10–13). In the process of doing that, they were completely missing the point about God's kingdom. Righteousness, peace and joy are what we should be pursuing, not rules about eating and drinking. Human relationships are much more important than food. Does this challenge any of your attitudes to other believers?

■ **PRAYER**

Father, help me to see any ways my attitudes to other Christians are wrong. Help me to focus on the peace and joy which your Holy Spirit gives. Amen

Isaiah 55:12–13 (NIV, abridged)

A joyful world

You will go out in joy and be led forth in peace; the mountains and hills will burst into song before you, and all the trees of the field will clap their hands... This will be for the Lord's renown, for an everlasting sign, that will endure forever.

'You shall go out with joy' was a very popular praise song in the 1970s and 1980s. It seemed as though we were always singing it. Do you remember it? It's a wonderful description of the return of God's people from exile in Babylon, pointing to the time when the whole of creation will be restored to God's original intention.

God's people – like us – had been disobedient and this had resulted in them going to exile in Babylon. But just as God had delivered them from Egypt, he was going to deliver them from Babylon. So there was every reason for 'going out in joy'. Similarly, God's plan for us is that we will know joy.

God's plan was also for them – and us – to know peace. When God puts everything right, it will lead to peace in the world. Our chaotic world will be put right. What a great hope.

■ **PRAYER**

Thank you, Father, that joy and peace are a part of your plan for us and for your world. May the way I live today demonstrate your plan to all those I meet. Amen

Bearing fruit

'Remain in me, as I also remain in you. No branch can bear fruit by itself; it must remain in the vine. Neither can you bear fruit unless you remain in me.'

JOHN 15:4 (NIV)

As a charity, BRF Ministries is always doing a huge assortment of things, from our Anna Chaplaincy team equipping people to minister to older people to our Messy Church team bringing Jesus to families across the world. From our Parenting for Faith ministry reaching parents and church leaders to transform ideas about how to raise God-connected children to our Living Faith resources that span so many different topics to help people to develop their faith journey.

At a glance these activities might seem distant or disparate but a closer look shows the vine from which all our ministries grow. The mission set out by Leslie Mannering over 100 years ago to which we still hold today: inspiring people of all ages to grow in faith. God is at the heart of all that we do and we are hugely thankful for all the fruits we have born through this work over the last century and more.

We want to keep building on this work, adapting, growing and finding even more glorious ways for people to grow in their faith while still remaining rooted to our mission.

This work would not be possible without kind donations from individuals, charitable trusts and gifts in wills. If you would like to support us now and in the future you can become a Friend of BRF Ministries by making a monthly gift of £2 a month or more – we thank you for your friendship.

Find out more at **brf.org.uk/donate** or get in touch with us on **01235 462305** or via **giving@brf.org.uk**.

Grandparenting brings new life and joy, and also the opportunity to walk spiritually alongside our grandchildren. In this book, Becky Sedgwick explores how grandparents can actively encourage and equip their grandchildren to meet and know God, offering tools and skills for the journey. Whatever your circumstances, God has positioned you to be a unique voice speaking into your grandchildren's lives, helping to nurture them into the reality of a relationship with the God who loves them.

Grandparenting for Faith
Sharing God with the children you love the most
Becky Sedgwick
978 1 80039 204 5 £9.99
brfonline.org.uk

Six-session course handbook
Creative arts workshop
Sermon starters
Bible studies
Meditations
Prayer walk

A church's guide
to exploring mortality

Death & Life

Joanna Collicutt
Jo Ind
Victoria Slater
Alison Webster

This research-based book includes all you need to plan and deliver a course enabling people – old or young, healthy or frail – to prepare practically, emotionally and spiritually for their last months on this earth. The course covers six topics: legal practicalities; life stories; funeral planning; physical aspects of dying; spiritual aspects of dying; and the life to come. It also offers a range of materials on the theme of living well in the light of mortality: a creative workshop, sermon starters, Bible studies, meditations and a set of prayer stations which combine to form a prayer walk.

Death and Life
A church's guide to exploring mortality
Joanna Collicutt, Jo Ind, Victoria Slater and Alison Webster
978 1 80039 283 0 £19.99
brfonline.org.uk

To order

Online: **brfonline.org.uk**
Telephone: **+44 (0)1865 319700**
Mon–Fri 9.30–17.00
Post: complete this form and send to the address below

Delivery times within the UK are normally 15 working days. Prices are correct at the time of going to press but may change without prior notice.

Title	Issue	Price	Qty	Total
Grandparenting for Faith		£9.99		
Death and Life		£19.99		
Bible Reflections for Older People (single copy)	May–Aug 2024	£5.55		
Bible Reflections for Older People (single copy)	Sep–Dec 2024	£5.55		

POSTAGE AND PACKING CHARGES			
Order value	UK	Europe	Rest of world
Under £7.00	£2.00		
£7.00–£29.99	£3.00	Available on request	Available on request
£30.00 and over	FREE		

Total value of books	
Donation	
Postage and packing	
Total for this order	

Please complete in BLOCK CAPITALS

Title .... First name/initials .... Surname ....

Address ....

.... Postcode ....

Acc. No. .... Telephone ....

Email ....

Method of payment

❏ Cheque (made payable to BRF) ❏ MasterCard / Visa

Card no. ☐☐☐☐ ☐☐☐☐ ☐☐☐☐ ☐☐☐☐

Expires end ☐M☐M ☐Y☐Y Security code ☐☐☐ Last 3 digits on the reverse of the card

We will use your personal data to process this order. From time to time we may send you information about the work of BRF Ministries. Please contact us if you wish to discuss your mailing preferences **brf.org.uk/privacy**

Registered with
FUNDRAISING REGULATOR

Please return this form to:

BRF Ministries, 15 The Chambers, Vineyard, Abingdon OX14 3FE | **enquiries@brf.org.uk**
For terms and cancellation information, please visit brfonline.org.uk/terms.

Bible Reading Fellowship is a charity (233280) and company limited by guarantee (301324) registered in England and Wales

BIBLE REFLECTIONS FOR OLDER PEOPLE **GROUP SUBSCRIPTION FORM**

All our Bible reading notes can be ordered online
by visiting **brfonline.org.uk/subscriptions**

The group subscription rate for *Bible Reflections for Older People* will be £16.65 per person until April 2025.

☐ I would like to take out a group subscription for .... (*quantity*) copies.

☐ Please start my order with the September 2024 / January 2025 / May 2025* issue.
(*delete as appropriate*)

Please do not send any money with your order. Send your order to BRF Ministries and we will send you an invoice.

Name and address of the person organising the group subscription:

Title .... First name/initials .... Surname...

Address...

.... Postcode ....

Telephone... Email...

Church...

Name and address of the person paying the invoice if the invoice needs to be sent directly to them:

Title .... First name/initials .... Surname...

Address...

.... Postcode ....

Telephone... Email...

Please return this form to:
BRF Ministries, 15 The Chambers, Vineyard, Abingdon OX14 3FE | **enquiries@brf.org.uk**
For terms and cancellation information, please visit brfonline.org.uk/terms.

Bible Reading Fellowship is a charity (233280) and company limited by guarantee (301324),
registered in England and Wales

ROP0224

BIBLE REFLECTIONS FOR OLDER PEOPLE INDIVIDUAL/GIFT SUBSCRIPTION FORM

To order online, please visit **brfonline.org.uk/subscriptions**

☐ I would like to take out a subscription (*complete your name and address details only once*)
☐ I would like to give a gift subscription (*please provide both names and addresses*)

Title .... First name/initials .... Surname ....

Address ....

.... Postcode ....

Telephone .... Email ....

Gift subscription name ....

Gift subscription address ....

.... Postcode ....

Gift message (*20 words max. or include your own gift card*):

....

....

Please send **Bible Reflections for Older People** beginning with the September 2024 / January 2025 / May 2025* issue (**delete as appropriate*):

(*please tick box*)	**UK**	**Europe**	**Rest of world**
Bible Reflections for Older People	☐ £21.15	☐ £28.35	☐ £32.40

Total enclosed £ .... (*cheques should be made payable to 'BRF'*)

Please charge my MasterCard / Visa with £ ....

Card no. ☐☐☐☐ ☐☐☐☐ ☐☐☐☐ ☐☐☐☐

Expires end ☐☐ ☐☐ Security code ☐☐ Last 3 digits on the reverse of the card

We will use your personal data to process this order. From time to time we may send you information about the work of BRF Ministries. Please contact us if you wish to discuss your mailing preferences **brf.org.uk/privacy**

Please return this form to:
BRF Ministries, 15 The Chambers, Vineyard, Abingdon OX14 3FE | **enquiries@brf.org.uk**
For terms and cancellation information, please visit brfonline.org.uk/terms.

Bible Reading Fellowship is a charity (233280) and company limited by guarantee (301324) registered in England and Wale

BROP0224